T0083143

BIRDLAND

A musical drama for soloists, unison voices, SATB chorus, and instrumental ensemble

Bob Chilcott

STORY AND TEXTS BY CHARLES BENNETT

VOCAL SCORE

MUSIC DEPARTMENT

OXFORD
UNIVERSITY PRESS

OXFORD
UNIVERSITY PRESS
Great Clarendon Street, Oxford OX2 6DP,
United Kingdom

Oxford University Press is a department of the University of Oxford.
It furthers the University's objective of excellence in research, scholarship,
and education by publishing worldwide. Oxford is a registered trade mark of
Oxford University Press in the UK and in certain other countries

© Oxford University Press 2020

Bob Chilcott and Charles Bennett have asserted their right under the Copyright,
Designs and Patents Act, 1988, to be identified as the Authors of this Work

Database right Oxford University Press (maker)

First published 2020

Impression: 1

All rights reserved. No part of this publication may be reproduced,
stored in a retrieval system, or transmitted, in any form or by any means,
without the prior permission in writing of Oxford University Press

A licence to perform this work in public must be obtained
from the publisher or its overseas agent as appropriate

Permission to make and exploit a recording of this work must be obtained
in advance from the Mechanical-Copyright Protection Society Ltd (MCPS)
at www.prsformusic.com or a local mechanical copyright licensing organization

Enquiries concerning reproduction outside the scope of the above
should be directed to the Music Rights Department, Oxford University Press,
at music.permissions.uk@oup.com or at the address above

ISBN 978-0-19-352300-5

Music and text origination by Andrew Jones

Printed in Great Britain on acid-free paper by
Halstan & Co. Ltd, Amersham, Bucks.

Contents

Dramatis Personæ iv
Composer's note v

Birdland

SCENE 1

1. Prologue (Pip, SATB Chorus Birds) 1
2. One Note (Unison Chorus Birds, SATB Chorus Birds) 4
3. Feathered Perfection (Highnote, Solo Birds) 13
4. You'll never believe it (Solo Bird, Unison Chorus Birds, SATB Chorus Birds) 16
5. I have a song (Pip, Unison Chorus Birds, SATB Chorus Birds, Highnote) 23
6. It's natural to dream (Highnote, Pip, SATB Chorus Birds) 28
7. Make that dream come true (Pip, Unison Chorus Birds) 34
8. Downwards (SATB Chorus Birds) 36

SCENE 2

9. The Bower of Power (Unison Chorus Birds, SATB Chorus Birds, Pip, Highnote, Solo Doc Rock Peacocks 1–5) 42
10. Time to move on (SATB Chorus Birds, Pip, Unison Chorus Birds, Solo Doc Rock Peacocks 1–3) 60

SCENE 3

11. Owl Talk (Wit, Woo, Croakencaw) 68

SCENE 4

12. The Bewilderness (Croakencaw, SATB Chorus Birds, Pip) 75

SCENE 5

13. Owl Talk again (Wit, Woo, Shamira, Pip) 81
14. Dream Vision (Shamira, Pip) 88
15. The Music of Light (Pip, Shamira, Unison Chorus Birds, SATB Chorus Birds, Highnote) 94
16. One Note (*reprise*) (Unison Chorus Birds, SATB Chorus Birds) 102
17. Epilogue (Pip) 108

Dramatis Personæ

Pip, a sparrow
Highnote, the Head Bird
Solo Birds 1–4
Solo Doc Rock Peacocks 1–5
Wit (Owl 1)
Woo (Owl 2)
Croakencaw, the Head of the Bewilderness
Shamira, the Golden Nightingale

Unison Chorus Birds
SATB Chorus Birds

All parts can be taken by a high treble voice. The parts of Highnote and Croakencaw can be taken by a high treble voice or a broken male voice.

Instrumentation

Flute
2 clarinets in B♭
Horn in F
Trumpet in B♭
Tenor trombone
Percussion (2 players)
Bass guitar (or double bass)
Piano

Also available:
Birdland Rehearsal Pack (ISBN 978–0–19–354015–6)

- Photocopiable unison part
- Photocopiable lyric sheets
- Access to a companion website, featuring downloadable audio rehearsal tracks and unison part and lyric sheets for printing

Composer's note

The poet Charles Bennett and I had for quite some time discussed the possibility of writing an extended dramatic work for young singers. Charles had the basis of the story in his mind, and we agreed that we wanted to write a piece not only about singing but also about what it means to have the courage to sing with your own voice, thus ultimately being true to who you really are. We were thrilled when Jon Cullen from Magdalen College School in Oxford, alongside Lucy Farrant from the Young Norfolk Arts Trust and Alison Corfield from Norfolk Music Hub, agreed to be partners with us by commissioning this piece. Thus *Birdland* came to life and received its first performances concurrently in the summer of 2020 at the Oxford Festival of the Arts and at the Young Norfolk Arts Festival, in Norwich Theatre Royal.

For us a major consideration was to make the piece as flexible for performance as we could. We have tried to make the solo roles interchangeable, in that they can be sung by any voice part. Even though the piece is fundamentally designed for young singers, the solo roles can equally be sung by adults or by young voices and adult voices combined. The work is scored for an ensemble of ten players, but it can also be performed with just piano or piano with the help of percussion and bass guitar or double bass. In the same way we have tried not to be too prescriptive about stage directions. Even though we have tried to imagine the temporal shape and pacing of the piece through the scoring and narrative, we hope that there will be plenty of scope for creative staging. We imagined that the piece could include dance and movement, from the possibility of an occasional dancing chorus to perhaps a more formal dance routine in movement eight, 'Downwards.' We hope that, ultimately, the nature of the piece might be able to stimulate and encourage as imaginative and broad a palette of ideas as possible, when bringing it to life.

As well as the commissioners, I would like to thank a number of colleagues who have helped this piece come to life. Thanks are due to Val Withams from Choral Connections and also to Griselda Sherlaw-Johnson and Jenny Wegg at Oxford University Press. I would especially like to thank our editor, Laura Jones, for her tireless work on this piece, not only for her careful work on the score but also for her masterminding of all the learning materials for the work, which she has done with grace, good humour, and endless patience.

Bob Chilcott
November 2019

Duration: *c.*45 mins

This note may be reproduced as required for programme notes.

BIRDLAND

Charles Bennett (b. 1954)

BOB CHILCOTT

1. Prologue

(Pip, SATB Chorus Birds)

SCENE 1—Early morning in Birdland. Pip is awake, standing centre stage.

© Oxford University Press 2019

Printed in Great Britain

OXFORD UNIVERSITY PRESS, MUSIC DEPARTMENT, GREAT CLARENDON STREET, OXFORD OX2 6DP

The Moral Rights of the Composer have been asserted. Photocopying this copyright material is ILLEGAL.

15
SATB CHORUS BIRDS emerge from sleep.
gave_ me a choice.
8va
19
S.
A.
SATB CHORUS BIRDS p
oo
T.
B.
p
oo
8va
23
PIP
PIP p
My fea - thers are brown,
but my
S.
A.
oo
T.
B.
oo

27
mp
song will dance in your ears to - night, if you
mp
oo
mp
oo
mp
31
Exit
give_ me a chance.
UNISON CHORUS BIRDS emerge from sleep.
8va
8va
p
attacca

2. One Note

(*Unison Chorus Birds, SATB Chorus Birds*)

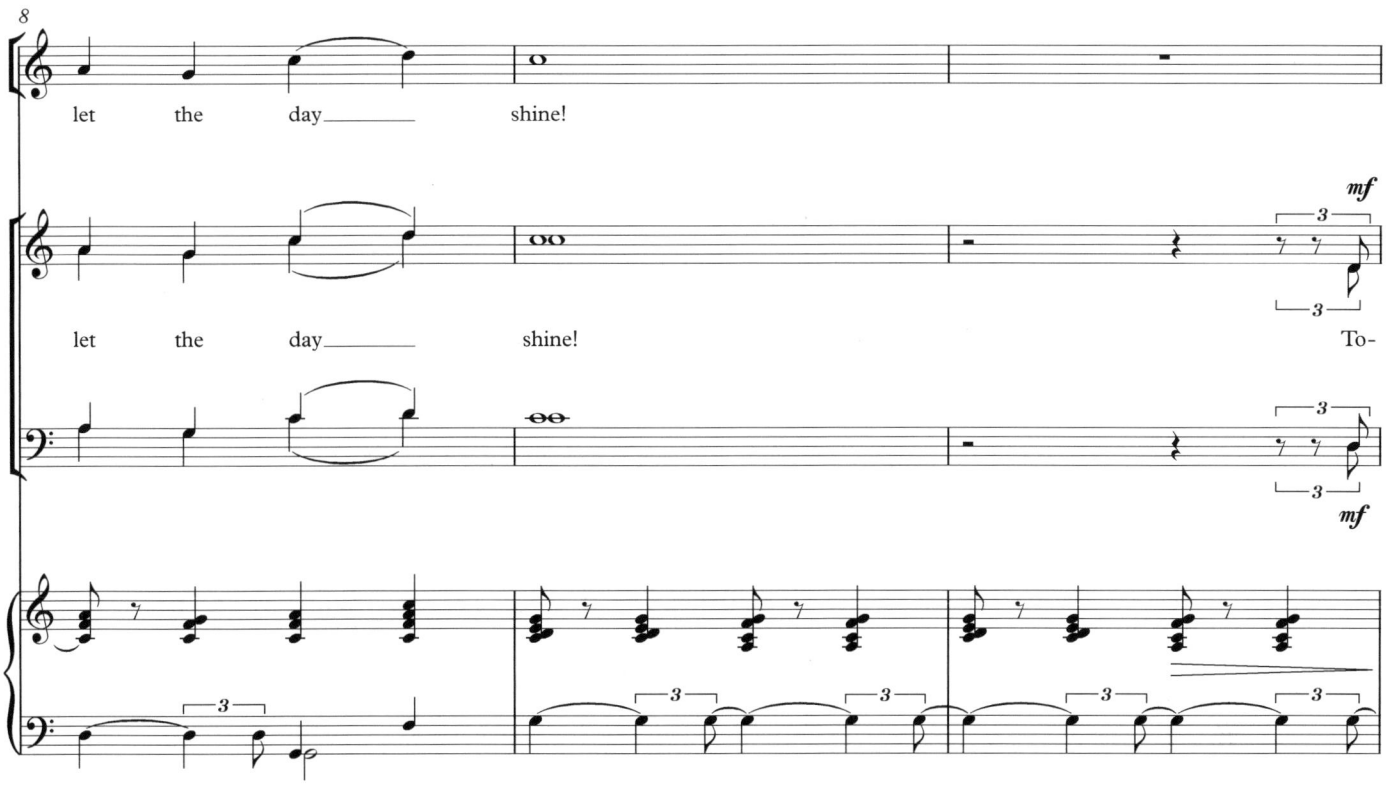
8
let the day shine!
let the day shine!
To-
mf
mf

11
- mor-row you know is Mid-sum-mer's Day, the ve - ry best birds will have their say.
But
f
f
mf

13
what can I tell you? Life is rough. Not ev - 'ry bird is good e-nough!
f

15
f
One note, to be-gin, let the light in. One note, now's the time,
One note, to be-gin, let the light in. One note, now's the time,

18
mf
let the day shine!
On
let the day shine!
21
UNISON VOICES
f
Mid-sum-mer's Day we'll sing at dawn a con - cert as the morn - ing's born.
But
mf
23
what can I tell you? Things are tough. Not ev - 'ry bird can strut their stuff!
f

25
UNIS.
One note, to be-gin, let the light in. One note, now's the time,
S.
A.
One note, to be-gin, let the light in. One note, now's the time,
T.
B.
28
let the day shine!
let the day shine!
mf
Se -

31
f
- lect - ed for a love - ly voice, the chor - us birds, the birds of choice. But
f
mf

33
what can I tell you? (Not a word.) There are birds, should not be heard!
f

35
f
One note, to be-gin, let the light in.
One note, to be-gin, let the light in.

37
One note, now's the time, let the day, the day shine!
One note, now's the time, let the day, the day shine!

40
ff
One note, to be-gin, let the light in.
ff
One note, to be-gin, let the light in.
ff
ff

42
One note, now's the time, let the day shine!
One note, now's the time, let the day shine!

45
Let the day shine, let the
Let the day shine, let the

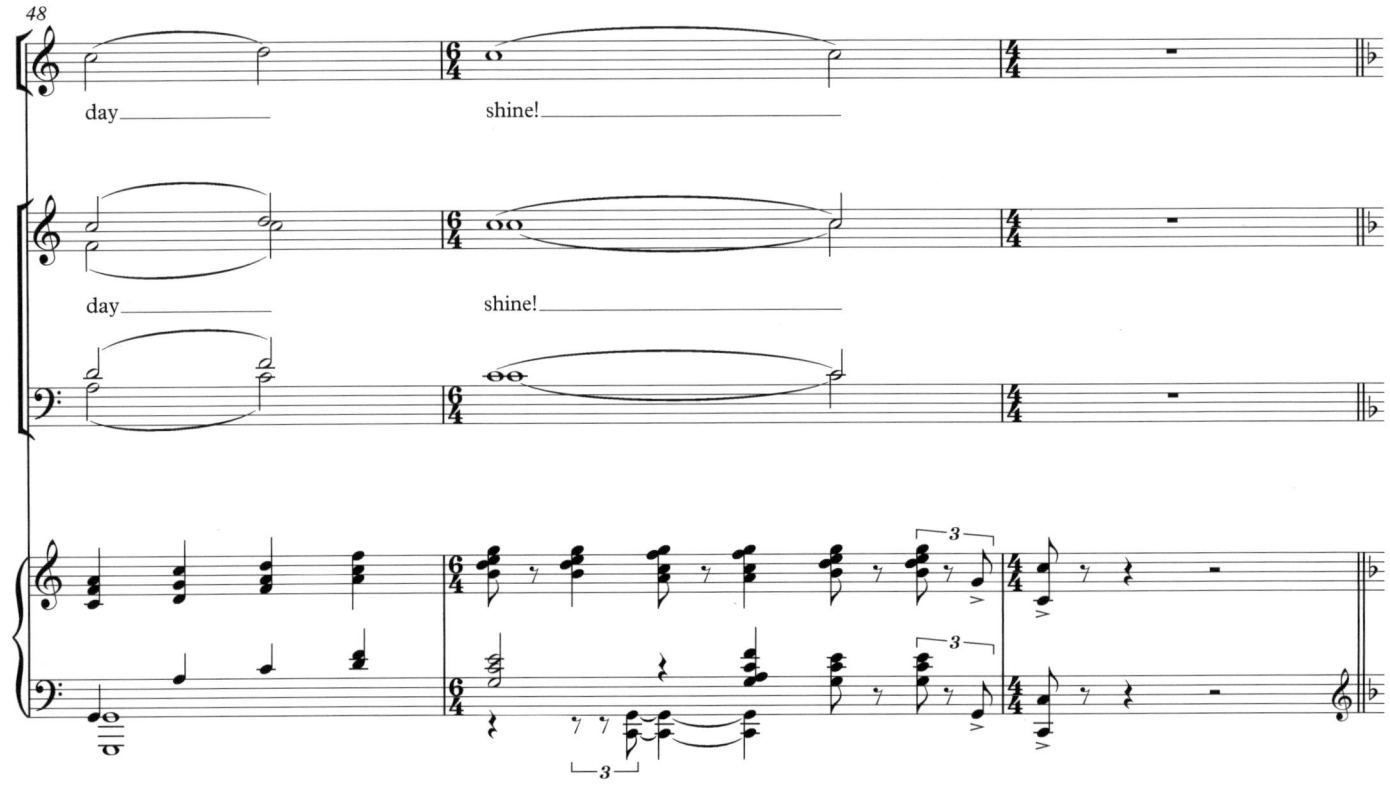
48
day shine!
day shine!

3. Feathered Perfection
(Highnote, Solo Birds)

23
SOLO BIRD 3
mf
It's not our fault we're the best.
SOLO BIRD 4
mf
It's the dream of ev - 'ry bird.
27
SOLO BIRDS 3 & 4
And that's us!
And that's us!
ALL SOLO BIRDS
We're
8va
32
fea-thered per - fec - tion,
And that's us!
8va
HIGHNOTE
"And remember, we have to make sure that our ineffable beauty of song keeps the wannabees and aspiring singers out of the running for ever.
36
8va
8va
p

42
Just one false note, one wrong step, one feather out of place
and aeons of natural selection would go up in smoke."
HIGHNOTE
mf
Be the best of the best.
8va
mf
48
ALL SOLO BIRDS
mf
Af-ter all, we have to be.
And that's us!
8va
52
f
And that's us!
We're fea-thered per - fec - tion,
f
56
we're per-fec - tion, fea-thered per - fec - tion,
And that's us!
8va

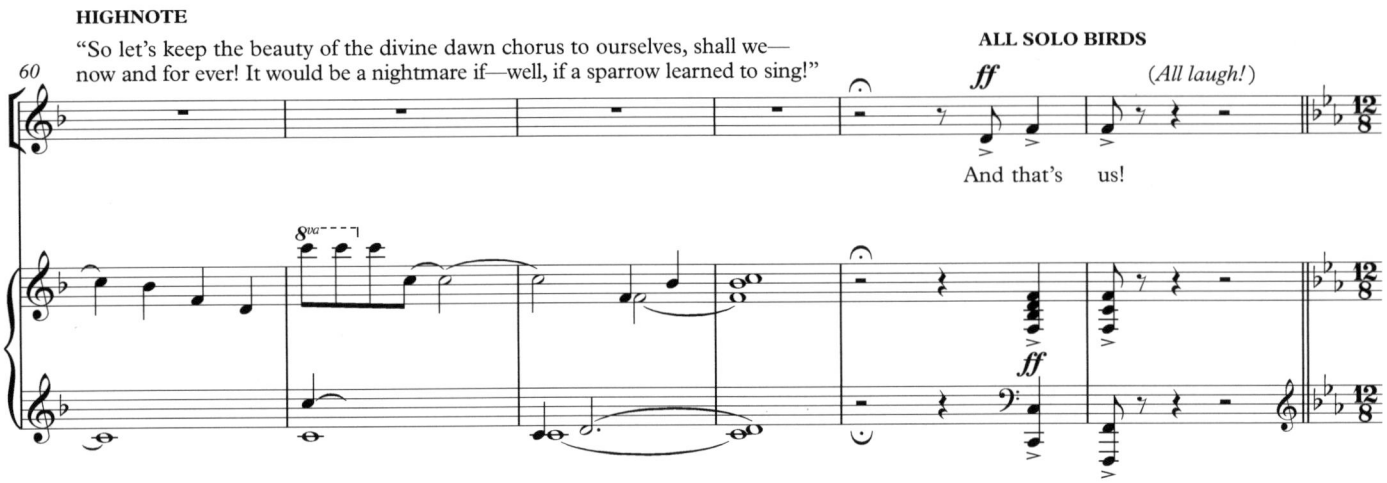

4. You'll never believe it

(Solo Bird, Unison Chorus Birds, SATB Chorus Birds)

8
I've ev - er had.
You'll ne - ver be - lieve it, here's the thing,
f
f
11
Dreamt last night
a spar - row could
mf
mf
mp
mp
14
S.
A.
sing.
SATB CHORUS BIRDS
mf
What's
T.
B.
mf
mf
18
that we heard? What's that you said?
Wish we were still a -

21
UNISON CHORUS BIRDS
UNIS.
You'll ne-ver be-lieve it, here's the thing,
S.
A.
- sleep in bed.
You'll ne-ver be-lieve it, here's the thing,
T.
B.
25
We all dreamt a spar - row could sing.
We all dreamt a spar - row could sing.
What

28
f
You'll
f
ah
ah
You'll
would it take to make us sane, to make our world com-plete a - gain?
f
31
ne-ver be-lieve it, here's the thing,
We dreamt we heard a
We dreamt we heard a
ne-ver be-lieve it, here's the thing,
We dreamt we heard, we

34
spar - row sing!
spar - row sing!
heard a spar - row sing!
sub. mf
38
mf
To - mor-row at dawn, you re - al - ise,
mf

41
(UNISON CHORUS BIRDS)
f
You'll
We sing our song to-ge - ther, we har - mon - ise.
You'll
45
ne-ver be-lieve it; Oh, the dread!
If a spar - row
ne-ver be-lieve it; Oh, the dread!
If a spar - row
f

48
sang in - stead. You'll ne-ver be-lieve it; Oh, the dread!
Oh, the dread!
sang in - stead. You'll ne-ver be-lieve it; Oh, the dread, the dread!
51
mf
mp
If a spar - row sang in - stead.
mf
mp
If a spar - row sang in - stead.
mf
mp
mf
mp
p

5. I have a song

(*Pip, Unison Chorus Birds, SATB Chorus Birds, Highnote*)

11
PIP "But this song. Inside me. Like this."
ff
ne - ver a-mount to a - ny-thing?
ff
ne - ver a-mount to a - ny-thing?
ff
ff
sub. p

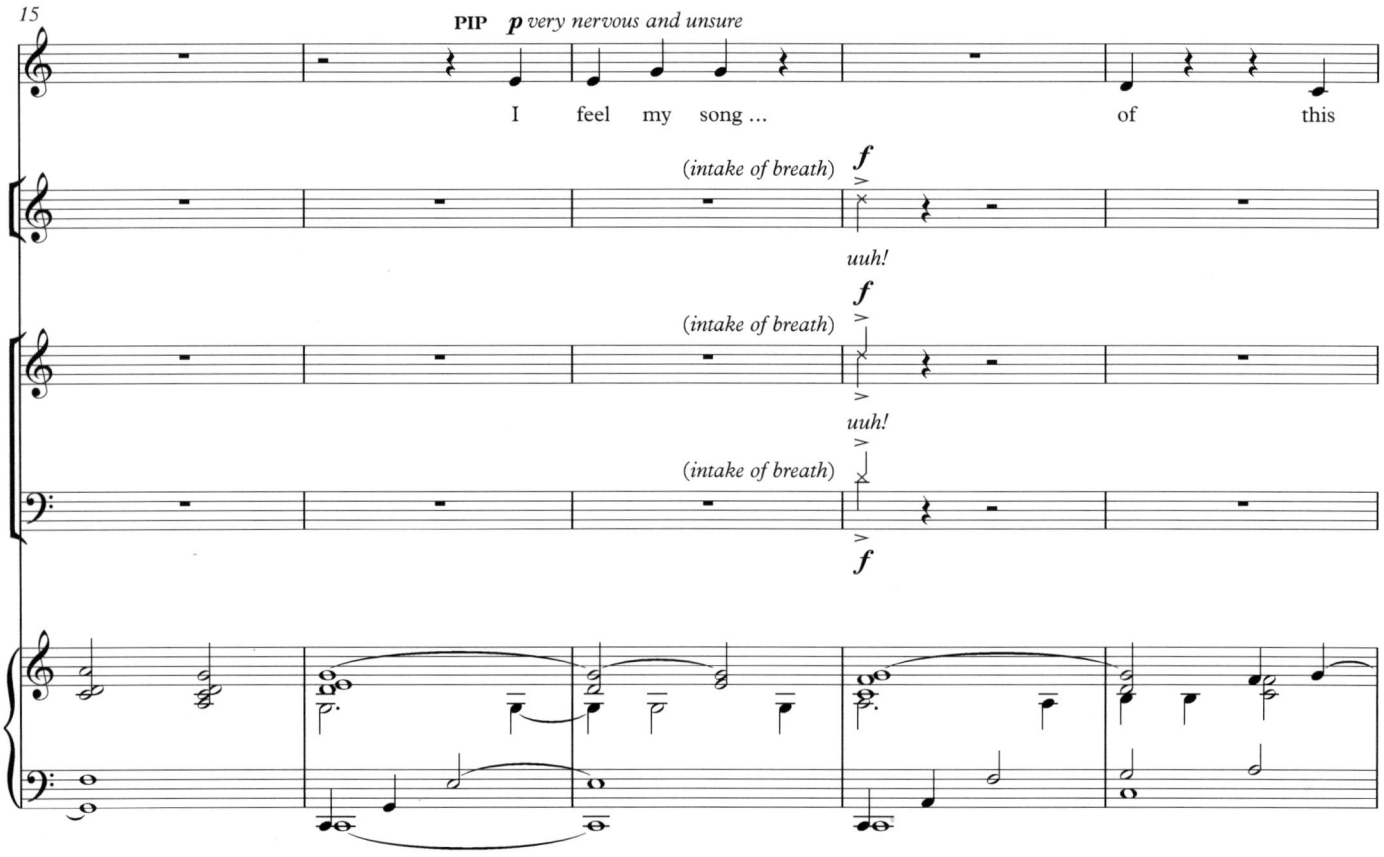
15
PIP p very nervous and unsure
I feel my song ... of this
(intake of breath) f
uuh!
f
(intake of breath)
uuh!
(intake of breath)
f

20
f
day ...
now at last ...
(shout)
NO!
(shout)
ff
Aaargh!
f
The ve - ry best part
(shout)
NO!
(shout)
ff
Aaargh!
f
The ve - ry best part
(shout)
(shout)
ff
f
f
25
mp
f
So let us all ...
ff
is the si - lence be - fore the start.
ff
is the si - lence be - fore the start.
ff
ff
mp

29
p
Like a fea - ther ...
(groan)
f
Oh!
(groan)
f
Oh!
(groan)
f
p
34
A song ... on the wind ...
(shout, aghast)
ff
HOR - ROR! THE SHOCK! NE - VER! AAARGH!
(shout, aghast)
ff
HOR - ROR! THE SHOCK! NE - VER! AAARGH!
(shout, aghast)
ff

39
f
No one must ev - er hear a sound so pain - ful, so pain - ful to the ear.
f
No one must ev - er hear a sound so pain - ful, so pain - ful to the ear.
f
f
ff
42
(shout)
NE - VER! NE - VER NE - VER NE - VER! NE - VER! NE - VER!
ff
No one must ev - er hear a sound so pain - ful, so pain - ful to the ear.
ff

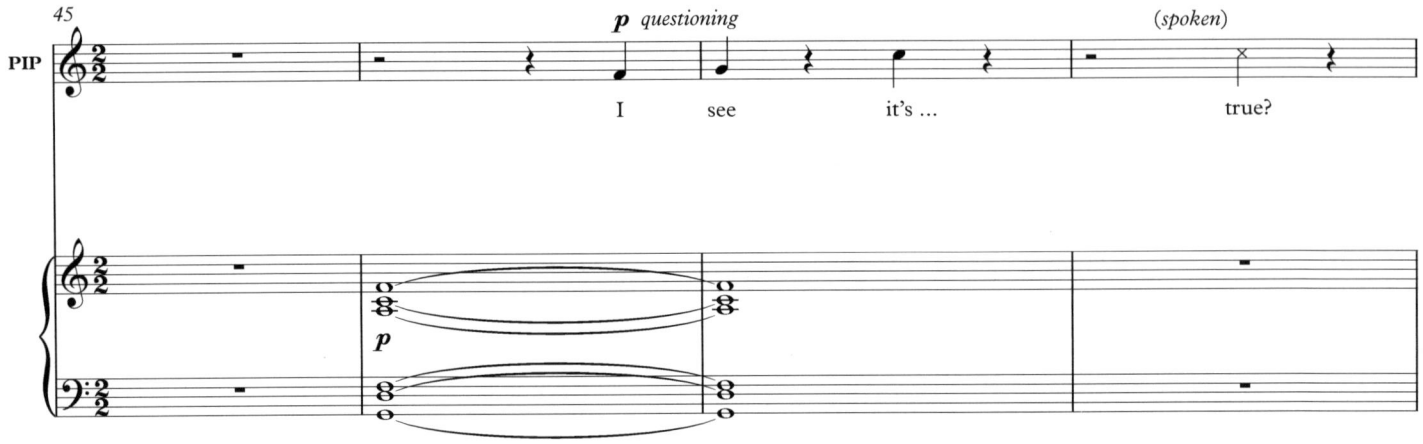

HIGHNOTE (*ripe with condescension, mock-friendly*)

"Come closer, my little, insignificant, tiny, small, inconsequential one. You've managed to achieve something quite extraordinary: a musical disaster of unprecedented proportions."

6. It's natural to dream

(*Highnote, Pip, SATB Chorus Birds*)

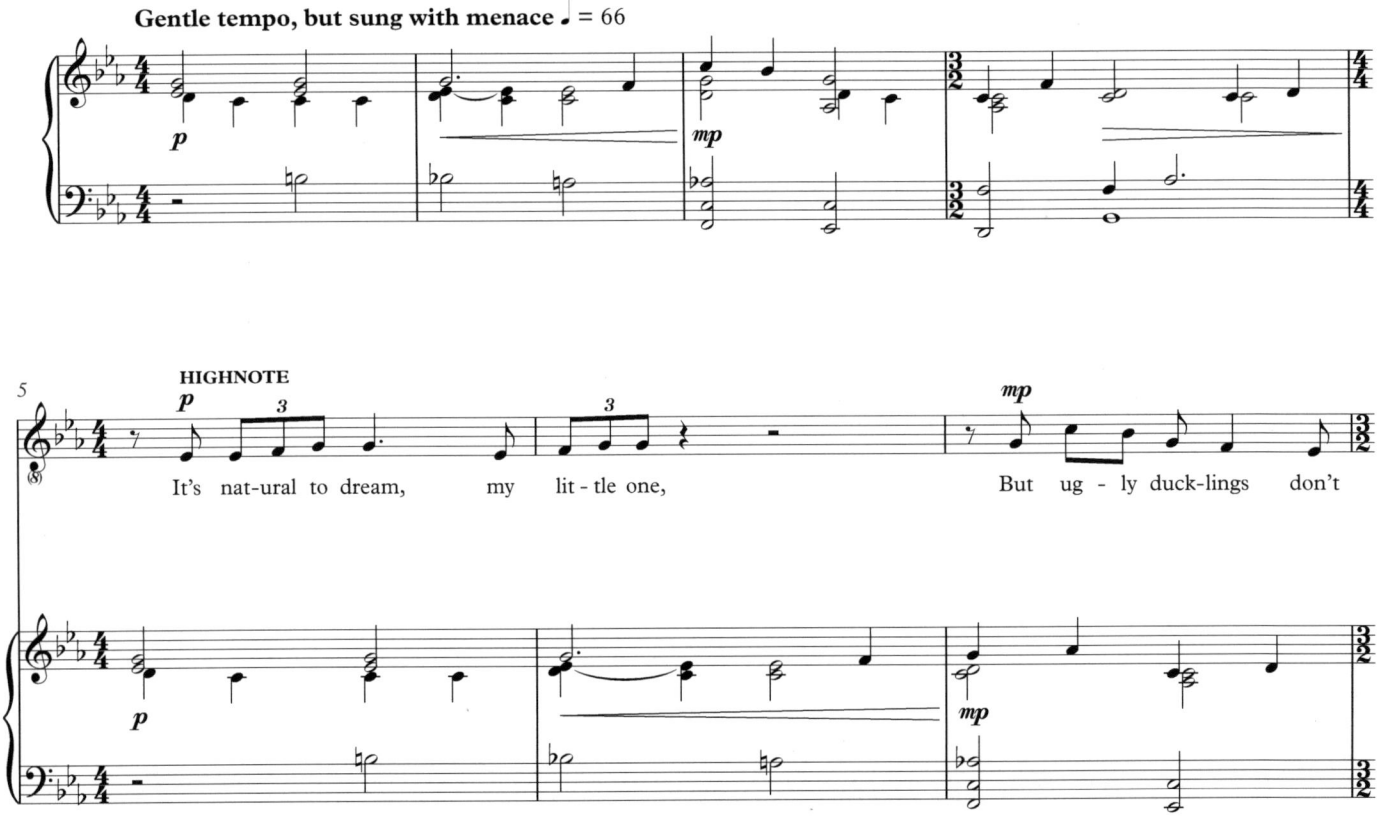

8
turn in - to swans.
And though we sym-pa-thise with you, my love, A
11
ra-ven ne-ver turns in - to a dove.
PIP
"All beginners make mistakes."
15
PIP
"I'll promise to do whatever it takes."
HIGHNOTE
You're not the first who wants to
SATB CHORUS BIRDS
S.
A.
T.
B.

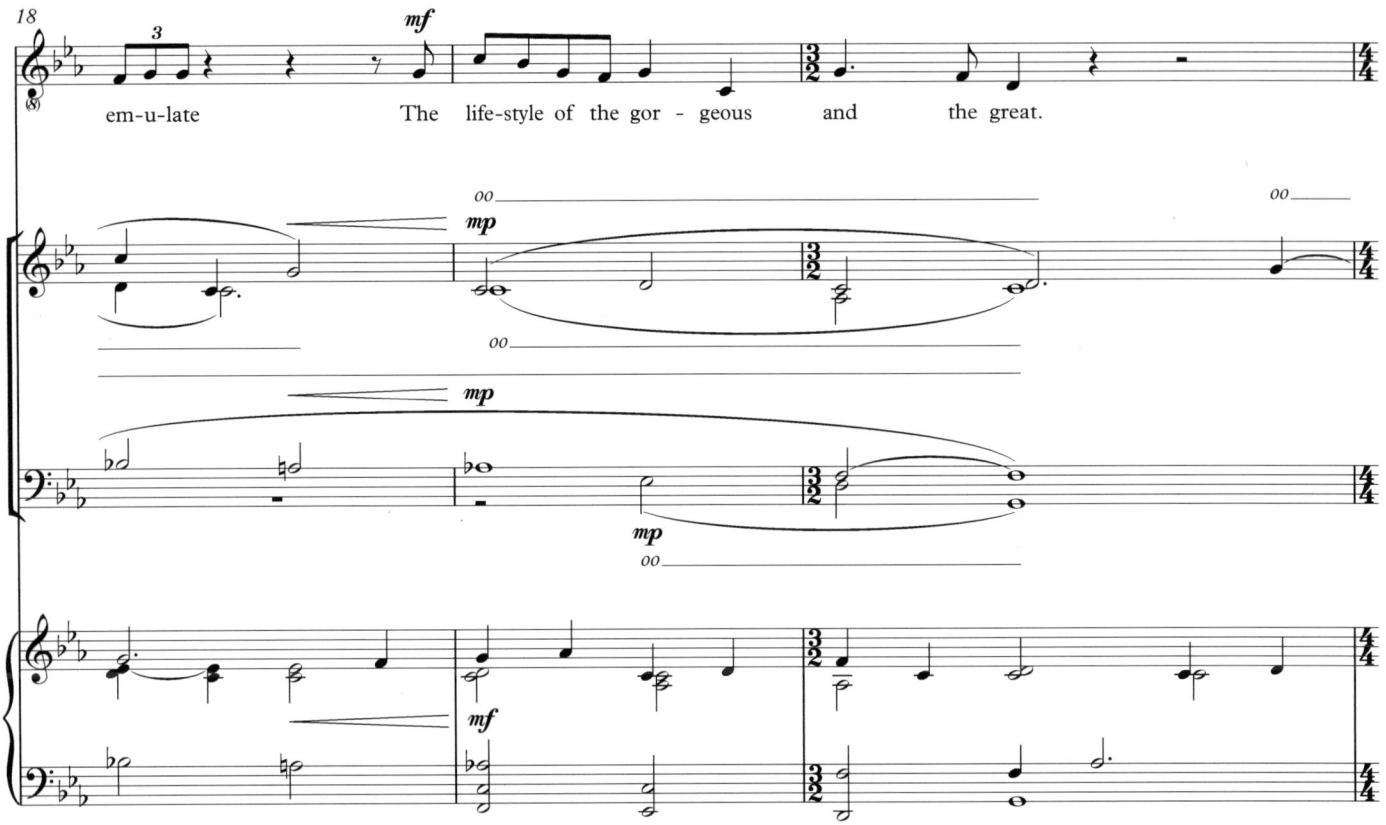
18
mf
em-u-late
The life-style of the gor - geous and the great.
mp
mp
mp
mf

21
But hon-est - ly, we have to tell you true: We'll sing, you do what-ev-er it is you do.

PIP
"I'll work all day and work all night.
Do anything to make it right."
25
f
29
S.
A.
Since you're so keen, there might be a way. It's hard and you will have to pay.
T.
B.
f
33
A chance for those who want to sing. It will cost you ev - 'ry - thing!

PIP
"If you give me the chance to shine, I'll give you everything that's mine!"
38
sub. p
HIGHNOTE
44
p
That's what I ra - ther hoped you'd say,
mp
p
48
mp
So just sign here with - out de - lay.
We'll see some friends of ours who'll make A
mf
mp

HIGHNOTE

"Don't mention it! It's my duty and my pleasure to take you where you can get the professional help you so very badly need, my little, tiny speck of easily overlooked, not-very-interesting dust."

PIP

"Thank you. Lovely.
Marvellous. Great. Where to?"

HIGHNOTE

"The Doc Rock Peacocks. You must have heard of them. They can fix any problem, great, or, as in your case, very, very small. They can build reputations and tear them down. They made Shamira, the Golden Nightingale, the fabled, block-busting star of stage and screen and national treasure she is today!"

7. Make that dream come true
(Pip, Unison Chorus Birds)

13
"Everyone adores her."
tune.
Ev - 'ry - one says she's great.
17
"The one I want to be like."
The one to em - u - late.
21
(PIP) "I dream of her at night."
HIGHNOTE
p
(I do_ too.)
PIP "I'd like to be as great as her."
Let's make that dream come true.
26
HIGHNOTE "My friends the Doc Rock Peacocks all have PhDs in things like singology, voice-breaking, and star-making. As it happens, they live down there, so let's deliver you into their hands. They're just what you need—when song goes wrong."

8. Downwards

(SATB Chorus Birds)

Journeying to the Bower of Power, the home of the Doc Rock Peacocks

13
oo
8va
8va
oo
mp
17
oo
oo
mp
oo
mp
mp
21
oo
8va
8va

25
mf
ah
ah
mf
ah
ah
mf
29
ah
ah
f
ah
ah
ah
ah
f
ah
f

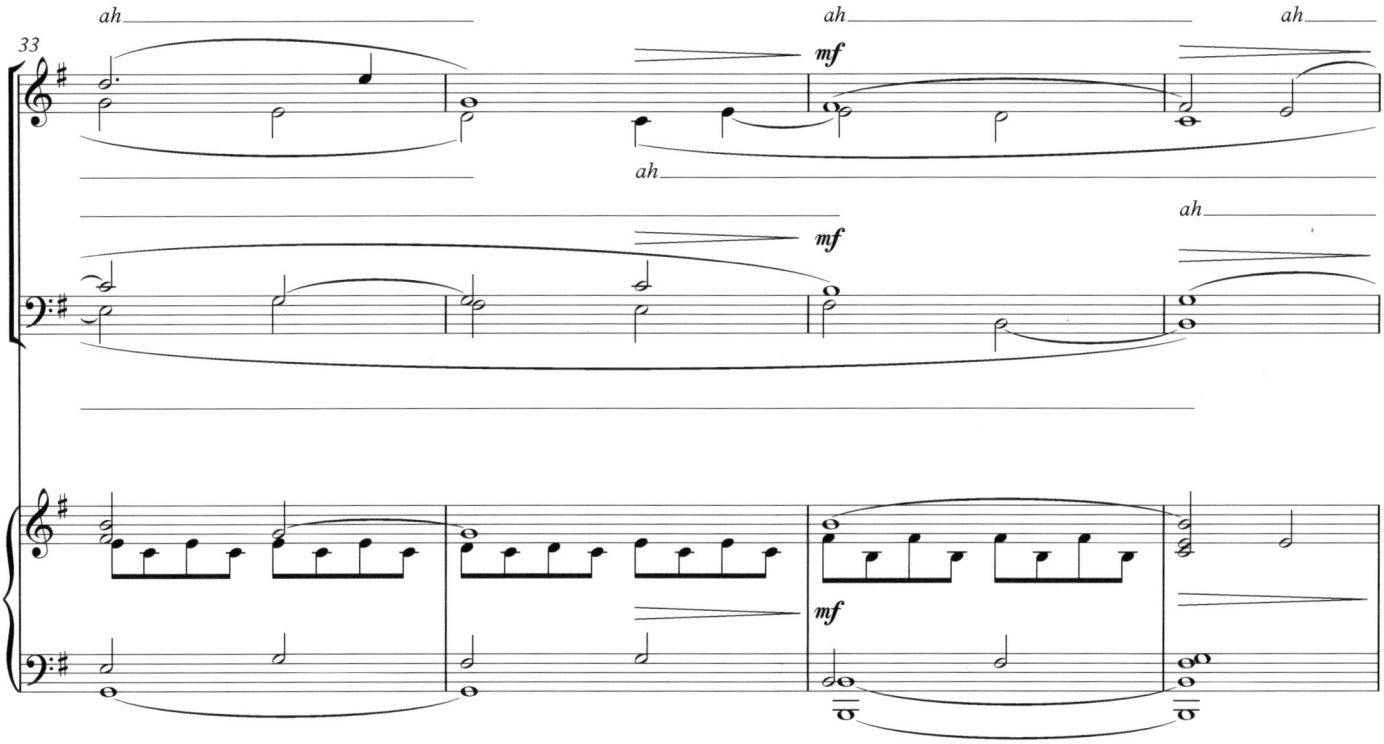
33
ah
ah
ah
mf
ah
mf
ah
mf

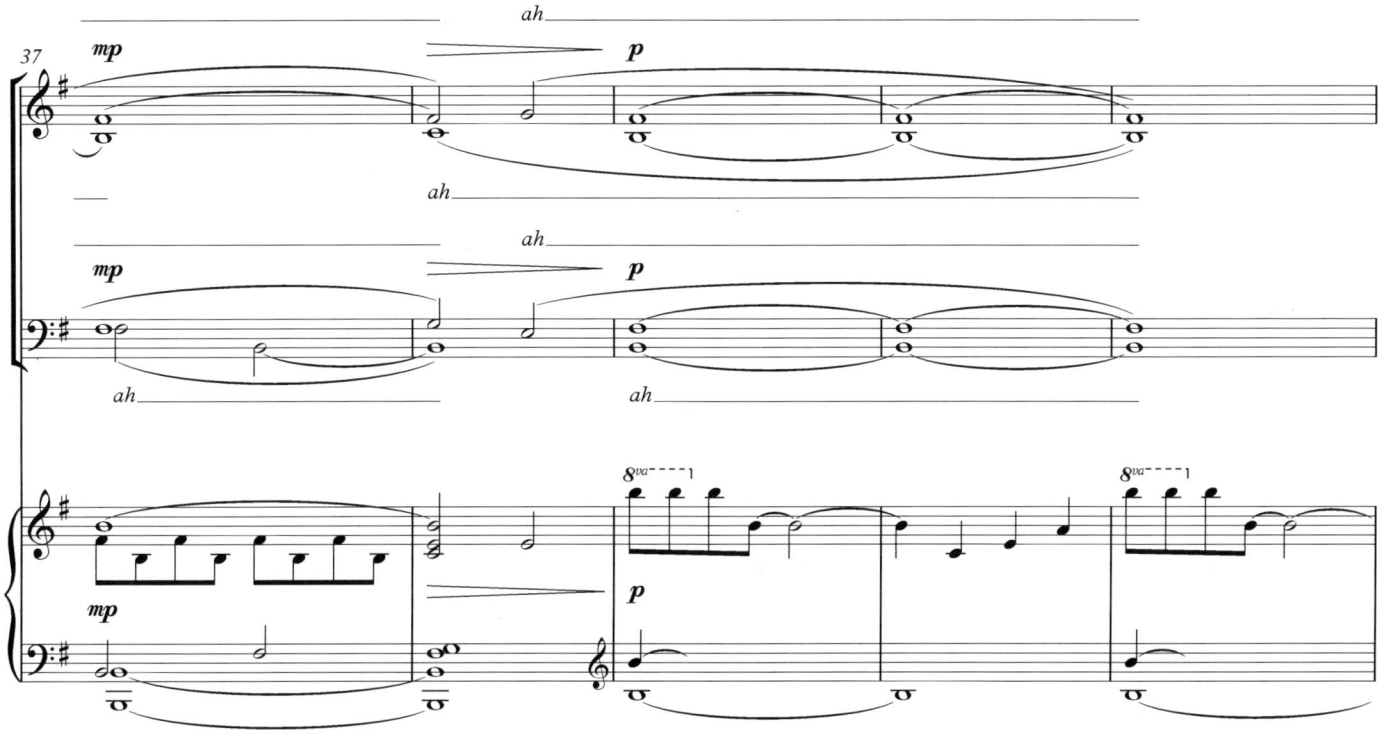
37
mp
ah
p
ah
mp
ah
p
ah
ah
8va
8va
mp
p

42
poco rit.
a tempo
8va
8va
47
S.
A.
oo
p espress.
oo
oo
T.
B.
p espress.
oo
51
oo
8va
8va

55
mp
mp
mp
59
p
p
p
8va
63
rit.
rit.
8va
8va

9. The Bower of Power

(Unison Chorus Birds, SATB Chorus Birds, Pip, Highnote, Solo Doc Rock Peacocks)

7
We can make it bet - ter, what - ev - er you're feel - ing. When
We can make it bet - ter, what - ev - er you're feel - ing. When
10
song goes wrong it's time to come a - long And let the Doc Rocks fix
song goes wrong it's time to come a - long And let the Doc Rocks fix

13
HIGHNOTE
"I've brought this little sparrow."
UNIS.
— you with a lit - tle bag of tricks!
S. A.
— you with a lit - tle bag of tricks!
T. B.
mp
16
PIP
"Hello, hello!"
HIGHNOTE
"He needs your special touch."
PIP
"So much, so much."
19
mf
S. A.
Tell a - bout your mo - ther, tell a - bout your pa. Tell us, lit - tle spar - row, just how
T. B.
mf
mf

22
sick you real - ly are. De - lu - sions such as yours are fan - tas - tic and u - nique. So lie
25
down on the couch, take the weight off your beak.
28
UNIS.
f
Wel - come to the Bower of Power. Wel - come to the place
S.
A.
unis. f
Wel - come to the Bower of Power. Wel - come to the place
T.
B.
unis.
f
f

31
of heal - ing. We can make it bet - ter, what - ev - er you're feel - ing.
of heal - ing. We can make it bet - ter, what - ev - er you're feel - ing.
34
When song goes wrong it's time to come a - long And
When song goes wrong it's time to come a - long And

* Repeat as necessary, following the narration.

"WE'LL TEAR YOU DOWN
AND BUILD YOU UP AGAIN!"
44
46 unis. mf
S.
A.
Af - ter all, dear spar - row, on your own you'd sure - ly fail
If you tried to war - ble like the
unis.
T.
B.
mf
mf
49
Gold - en Night - in - gale.
She's our great - est tri - umph, our o - ver - night suc - cess.
The

52
hair, the eyes, the lips, the dress!
55
UNIS.
f
Wel-come to the Bower of Power. Wel-come to the place
S.
A.
unis. f
Wel-come to the Bower of Power. Wel-come to the place
T.
B.
unis.
f
f

58
of heal - ing. We can make it bet - ter, what - ev - er you're feel - ing.
of heal - ing. We can make it bet - ter, what - ev - er you're feel - ing.
61
When song goes wrong it's time to come a - long And
When song goes wrong it's time to come a - long And

64
let the Doc Rocks fix you with a lit - tle bag of
let the Doc Rocks fix you with a lit - tle bag of
67
PIP
"Perhaps I might just ..."
DOC ROCK PEACOCK 2
"Take the next step. Certainly. You're sure? We'll pry and probe and make you what you never were before. We'll break you and remake you in an image of our own."
x 2
UNIS.
tricks!
S.
A.
tricks!
T.
B.
mp

ALL DOC ROCK PEACOCKS
"THEY WON'T RECOGNISE YOU BACK HOME!"
71
73 unis. mf
S.
A.
Now let's have a look at you: has - n't he done well! Trans - formed com-plete - ly
unis.
T.
B.
mf
mf
76
un - der our spell. There's just a few more things to rem - ed - y and tweak: The

79
hair, the legs, the mind, the beak!
82
UNIS.
f
Wel-come to the Bower of Power. Wel-come to the place
S.
A.
unis. f
Wel-come to the Bower of Power. Wel-come to the place
T.
B.
unis.
f
f

85
of heal - ing. We can make it bet - ter, what - ev - er you're feel - ing.
of heal - ing. We can make it bet - ter, what - ev - er you're feel - ing.

88
When song goes wrong it's time to come a - long And
When song goes wrong it's time to come a - long And

* Repeat as necessary, following the narration.

ALL DOC ROCK PEACOCKS
98
"WE'RE GOING TO REMOVE YOUR VERY SOUL!"
100
UNIS.
f
Wel-come to the Bower of Power. Wel-come to the place
S.
A.
f
Wel-come to the Bower of Power. Wel-come to the place
T.
B.
f
f

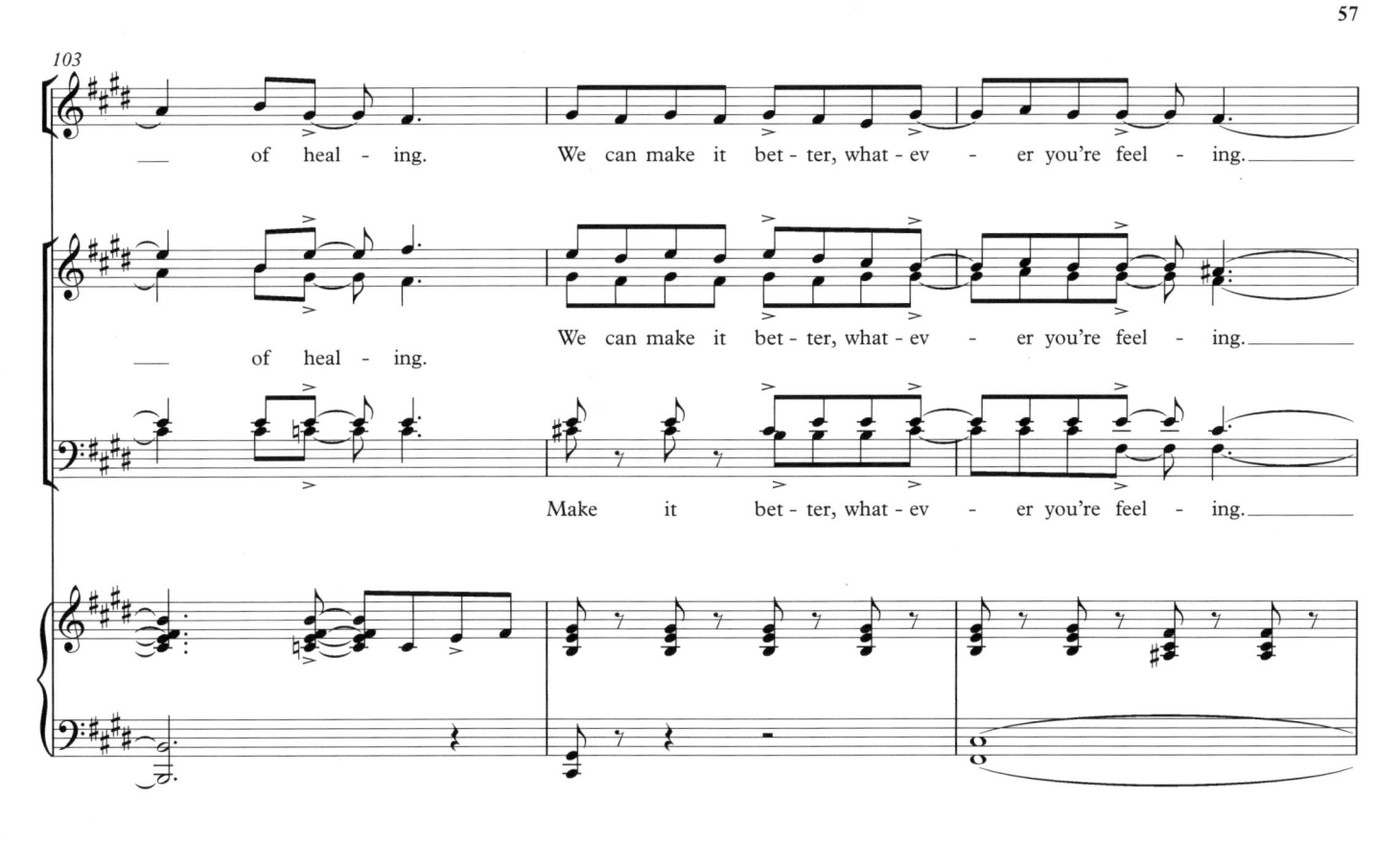
103
of heal - ing. We can make it bet - ter, what - ev - er you're feel - ing.
We can make it bet - ter, what - ev - er you're feel - ing.
of heal - ing.
Make it bet - ter, what - ev - er you're feel - ing.

106
When song goes wrong it's time to come a - long And
When song goes wrong it's time to come a - long And

109
1.
let the Doc_ Rocks fix___ you, fix you.
let the Doc_ Rocks fix___ you, fix you.
1.

111b
2.
ff
with a lit - tle bag of tricks!
ff
with a lit - tle bag of tricks!
ff
2.
ff

Steady (Menacing) ♩ = 63
113
DOC ROCK PEACOCK 1
mf
I've ne - ver known a soul so re - sist - ant.
DOC ROCK PEACOCK 2
mf
I've ne - ver known a mad-ness more per-
mf
115
DOC ROCK PEACOCK 3
mf
-sist - ent. We've tried the pli - ers, tried the knife,
DOC ROCK PEACOCK 4
mf
And still his soul clings
117
DOC ROCK PEACOCK 5
f
on for life. Ham-mer, chain - saw, J C B,
f
ALL DOC ROCK PEACOCKS
ff
RIP OUT THE
119
fff
SOUL AND GIVE IT TO ME!
(scream!)
AAARGH!
ff
fff
8vb

10. Time to move on

(SATB Chorus Birds, Pip, Unison Chorus Birds, Solo Doc Rock Peacocks 1–3)

9
Time to move on to some - thing new.
12
PIP
mp
In my dreams I sang so fair. I heard my mu - sic
15
ev - 'ry-where.
mf
But this is-n't right, this is - n't true.
mf

18
PIP
Time to move on to some - thing new.
UNIS.
mf
Time to move on to some - thing new.
S.
A.
mf
Time to move on to some - thing new.
T.
B.
mf

20
S.
A.
You'll ne-ver do it on your own.
T.
B.

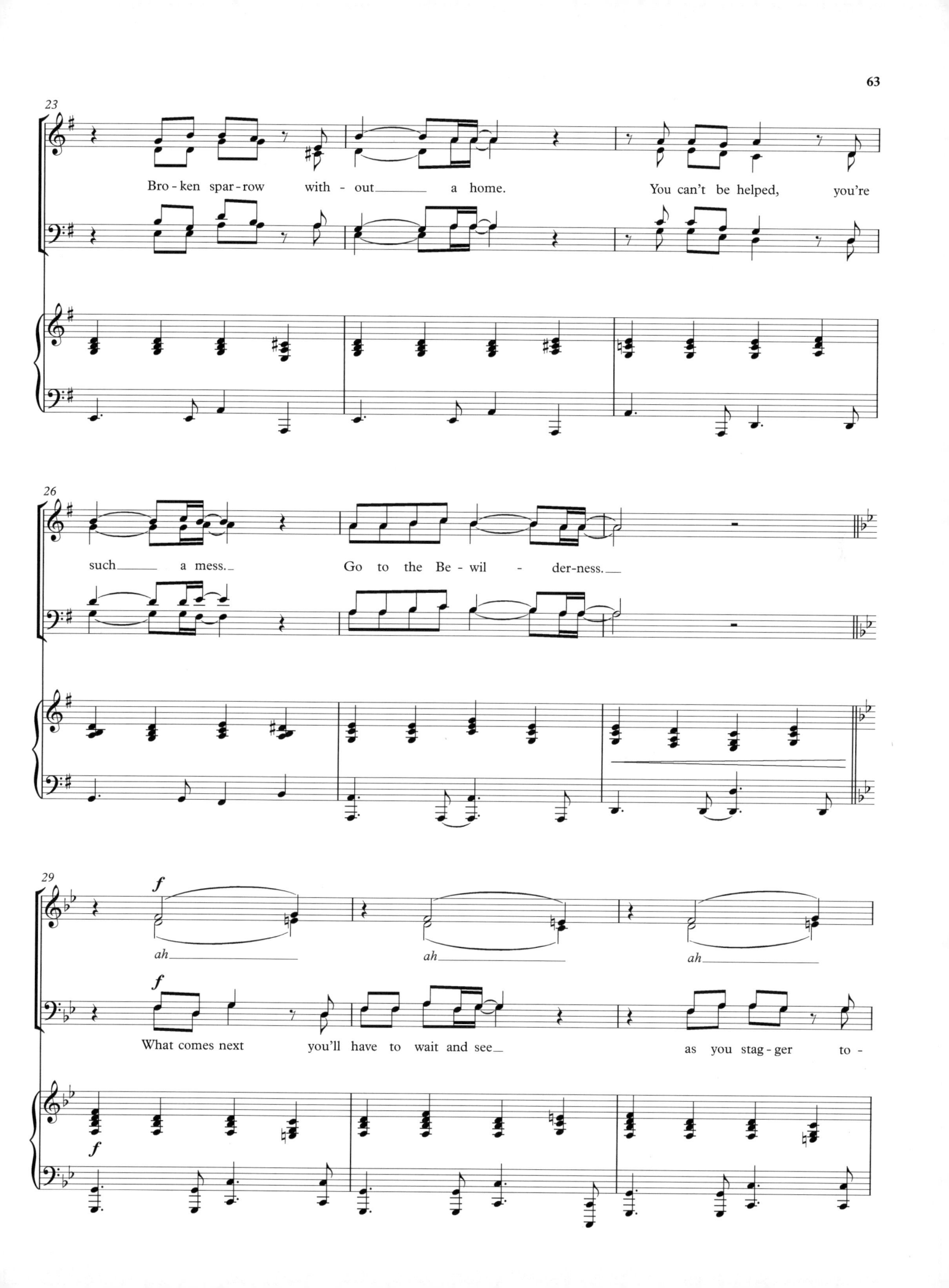
23
Bro - ken spar - row with - out a home.
You can't be helped, you're
26
such a mess.
Go to the Be - wil - der-ness.
29
f
ah
ah
ah
f
What comes next you'll have to wait and see
as you stag - ger to -
f

32
ah
-wards your des - ti - ny.
Now there is no - thing more we can do.
35
f
UNIS.
Time to move on to some - thing new.
S.
A.
Time to move on to some - thing new.
T.
B.

38
risoluto
S.
A.
Your life does not mean a thing. You are the bird, the
T.
B.
risoluto
risoluto
41
bird who could not sing. You can't be helped, you're such a mess.
44
ff
Go to the Be - wil - der-ness, Go to the Be - wil - der-ness,
ff
ff

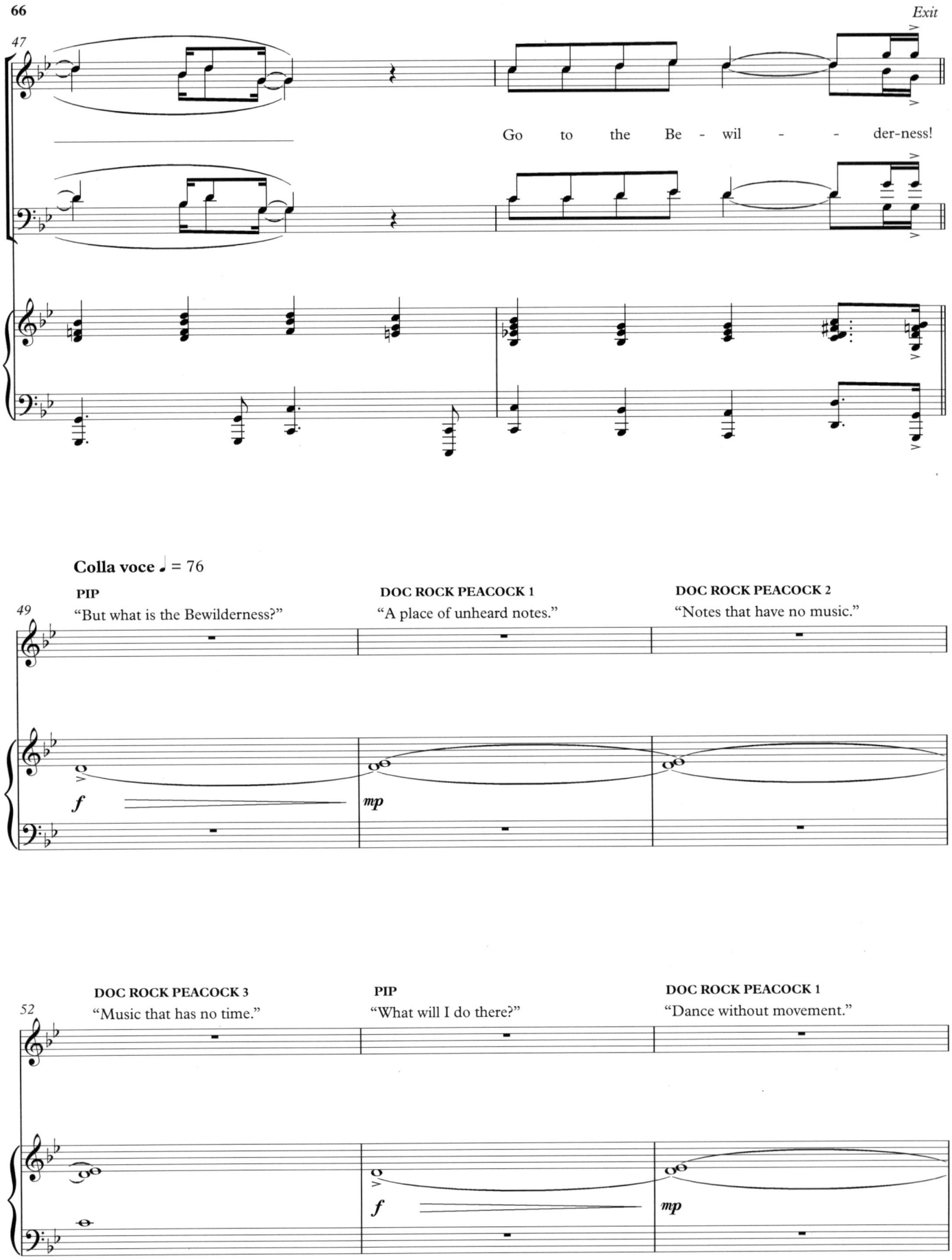
Exit
47
Go to the Be - wil - - der-ness!
Colla voce ♩ = 76
49
PIP
"But what is the Bewilderness?"
DOC ROCK PEACOCK 1
"A place of unheard notes."
DOC ROCK PEACOCK 2
"Notes that have no music."
f
mp
52
DOC ROCK PEACOCK 3
"Music that has no time."
PIP
"What will I do there?"
DOC ROCK PEACOCK 1
"Dance without movement."
f
mp

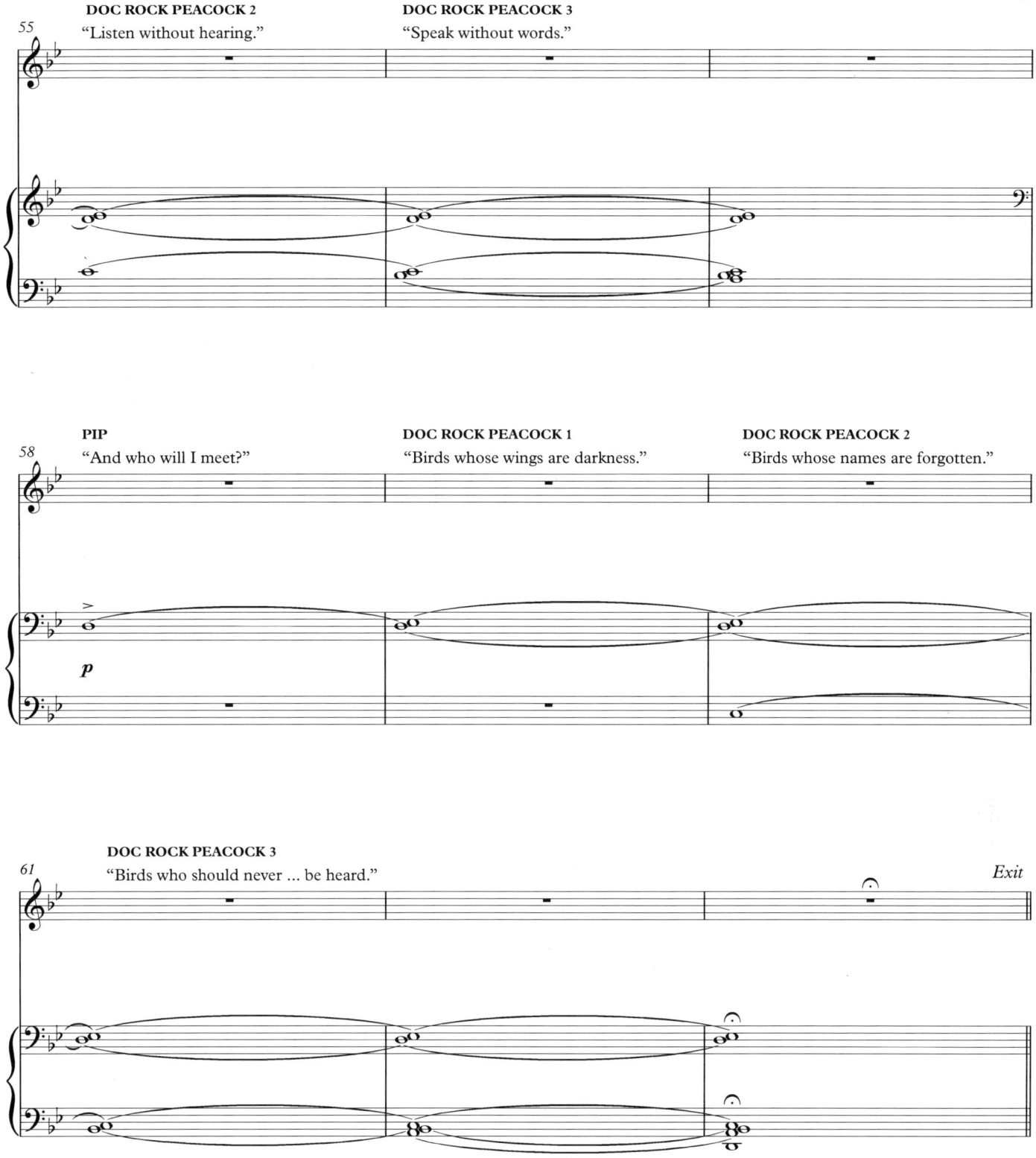

PIP

"Is what I wanted so wrong? To sing my own song. Is there a way to make it clear? The notes I hear? How can what's inside of me see the light of day? I thought I had music. Has it gone away?"

11. Owl Talk

(Wit, Woo, Pip, Croakencaw)

8
-'ry.
Keep it close
-'ry.
To your heart,
11
Ne-ver let it
In the end
A song_ might come your
Break a-part.
Who can say? A song_ might come your
14
PIP
"Oh Owls! It's all gone wrong!"
PIP
WIT
way.
WOO
way.
mp

18
PIP
"It's kind of you to say so.
mp
Dark-est night.
It just might
mp
Not gone right.
See the light.
21
(PIP)
"But right now I have to find my way to the Bewilderness.
And I don't even know how to get there."
23
WIT
That's the thing.
All you have to do
WOO
Find-ing it.
Is to feel com-plete-ly lost,

26
And the Be - wil - der - ness Comes to you!
Comes to you!
PIP
29
"Well, I feel utterly lost! It's all hopeless. Now I'll never sing like the Golden Nightingale."
WIT
31
"Oh, we know a thing or two about her."
"Things that would make you see her ..."
WOO
"Oh yes. We could tell you things that would blow your wings off."
"... In a totally different light."
(WIT)
35
"We saw how the Doc Rock Peacocks made her!"
mf

38
(WIT) mf
She has a se-cret We saw them make her blow by blow.
(WOO) mf
We both know, We saw them make her blow by blow.
41
Be - fore she was a night - in - gale.
We know who she was as well Be - fore she was a night - in - gale.
44
"We knew her when ..."
"... Nobody."
"She was just a ..."
"The Doc Rock Peacocks took her."

47
Dressed her up. Gave her a name. Gave her her fame. But we knew what she used to be.
Broke her down. Gave her a name. Gave her her fame.
50
Her se-cret i-den - ti - ty.
Her se-cret i-den - ti - ty.
54
"And maybe now's the time."
"We can bend your ears ..."
"Now's the place."
"... with what we've known for years."
mp

CROAKENCAW
"Hello, hello, hello. What stranger have we here?"

PIP
"Only a sparrow who thought he could sing. Only a sparrow with a broken wing."

CROAKENCAW
"Come with me. You'll fit in beautifully down here. Where the forest is dark and drear. Where your dreams don't mean a thing. You're the bird who could not sing."

12. The Bewilderness

(Croakencaw, SATB Chorus Birds, Pip)

SCENE 4—The Bewilderness.

Heavy and dark ♩ = 72

CROAKENCAW "The Bewilderness finds everyone like us in the end. The croakers, the broken, the rotten, the forgotten."

SOPRANO
ALTO

TENOR
BASS

Heavy and dark ♩ = 72

p

5

CROAKENCAW "It takes us when no one else will."

PIP "But who are you, and what do you call yourselves?"

"Birds who made bad choices."

p soulfully

woo

woo

p soulfully

CROAKENCAW
9
"Birds whose names are dirty words.
Birds who should never ... be heard."
mp
woo
woo
mp
mp
13
S.
A.
T.
B.
woo
Ev -'ry-thing that's
16
din - gy,
ev -'ry-thing that's drear,
Ev -'ry-thing that's bro - ken
winds up

* 'Maggot pie' = magpie

28
f
oo
'Hoo-ray!'
Please for-give our
f
jay.
With our voice of dark-ness
we will croak 'Hoo-ray!'
Please for-give our
f
31
man-ners,
please for-give the mess.
This is how we live in the Be-wil-der-
34
-ness.
You, my cra-zy spar-row, have been ban-ished here.

37
mf
With our voice of dark-ness, we will raise a cheer.
Fail-ures such as you add to
mf
mf
40
f
our suc-cess.
Soon you'll learn to live in the Be - wil - der-ness, Be -
f
f
43
p
-wil - der-ness.
woo
p
sub. p

46
mp
woo
You'll fit in so nice-ly,
we love the ab-
mp
mp
49
mf
- surd.
We are all the birds
who should ne-ver be heard.
Make your-self at
mf
mf
52
mp
home here
'cos you'll ne-ver guess
how we love to live in the Be-wil - der - ness,
mp
mp

13. Owl Talk again

(Wit, Woo, Shamira, Pip)

SCENE 5—The Forest. Night. Pip comes centre stage and sleeps.

Simple and clear ♩ = 88

WIT

WOO

Simple and clear ♩ = 88

p

5

9
WIT p
Poor old Pip,
Un-der-neath the song-less skies.
He
WOO p
Now he lies
12
does-n't know
has been in-side him all a-long.
That his song has been in-side him all a-long.
15
Poor old Pip,
He's for-got-ten how to rest.
So dis-tressed.

18
He's for - got - ten
Al - ways to your - self be true.
What he knew:
Al - ways to your - self be true.
21
mp
Poor old
mp
24
Pip, if he found the se - cret of the Night - in - gale's sound

27
that
mp
He might just un - do the spell that
30
rit.
holds her cap-tive to her - self.
holds her cap-tive to her - self.
rit.
p
A little slower ♩ = 76
34
p
Poor old Pip. Just stay true. To the song in - side of you.
p
Poor old Pip. Just stay true. To the song in - side of you.
A little slower ♩ = 76

37
And the night - in - gale could be fi - nal - ly, com - plete - ly
"Free"
And the night - in - gale could be fi - nal - ly, com - plete - ly
"Free"
42
WIT
"Wake up, Pip."
WOO
"Time to reflect ..."
WIT
"... on what to keep ..."
WOO
"... and what to reject ..."
44
WIT
"Wake up, Pip."
WOO
"Time to decide ..."
WIT
"... on the dream ..."
WOO
"... that waits inside."

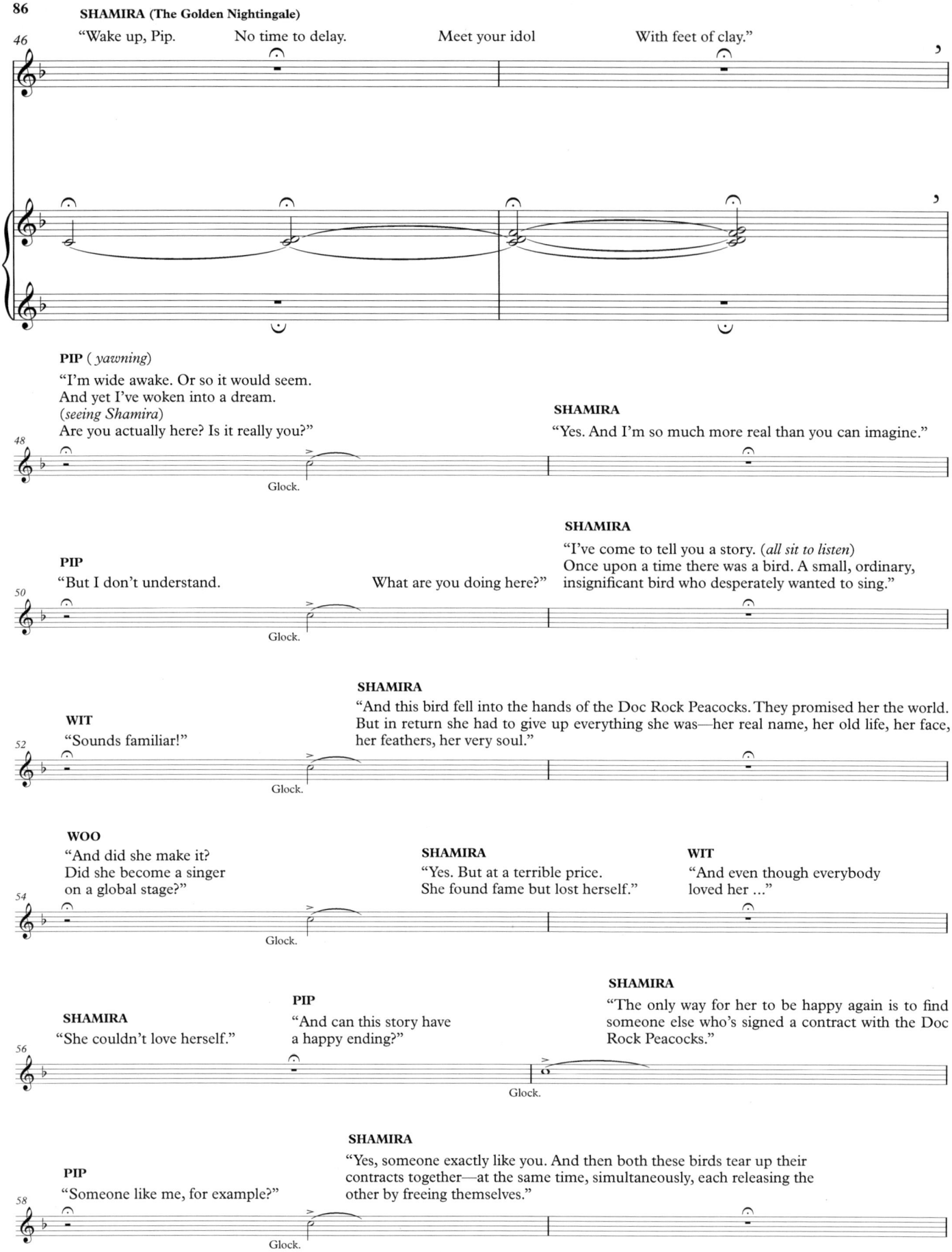
SHAMIRA (The Golden Nightingale)
"Wake up, Pip. No time to delay. Meet your idol With feet of clay."
46
PIP (yawning)
"I'm wide awake. Or so it would seem.
And yet I've woken into a dream.
(seeing Shamira)
Are you actually here? Is it really you?"
SHAMIRA
"Yes. And I'm so much more real than you can imagine."
48
Glock.
PIP
"But I don't understand. What are you doing here?"
SHAMIRA
"I've come to tell you a story. (all sit to listen)
Once upon a time there was a bird. A small, ordinary,
insignificant bird who desperately wanted to sing."
50
Glock.
WIT
"Sounds familiar!"
SHAMIRA
"And this bird fell into the hands of the Doc Rock Peacocks. They promised her the world.
But in return she had to give up everything she was—her real name, her old life, her face,
her feathers, her very soul."
52
Glock.
WOO
"And did she make it?
Did she become a singer
on a global stage?"
SHAMIRA
"Yes. But at a terrible price.
She found fame but lost herself."
WIT
"And even though everybody
loved her ..."
54
Glock.
SHAMIRA
"She couldn't love herself."
PIP
"And can this story have
a happy ending?"
SHAMIRA
"The only way for her to be happy again is to find
someone else who's signed a contract with the Doc
Rock Peacocks."
56
Glock.
PIP
"Someone like me, for example?"
SHAMIRA
"Yes, someone exactly like you. And then both these birds tear up their
contracts together—at the same time, simultaneously, each releasing the
other by freeing themselves."
58
Glock.

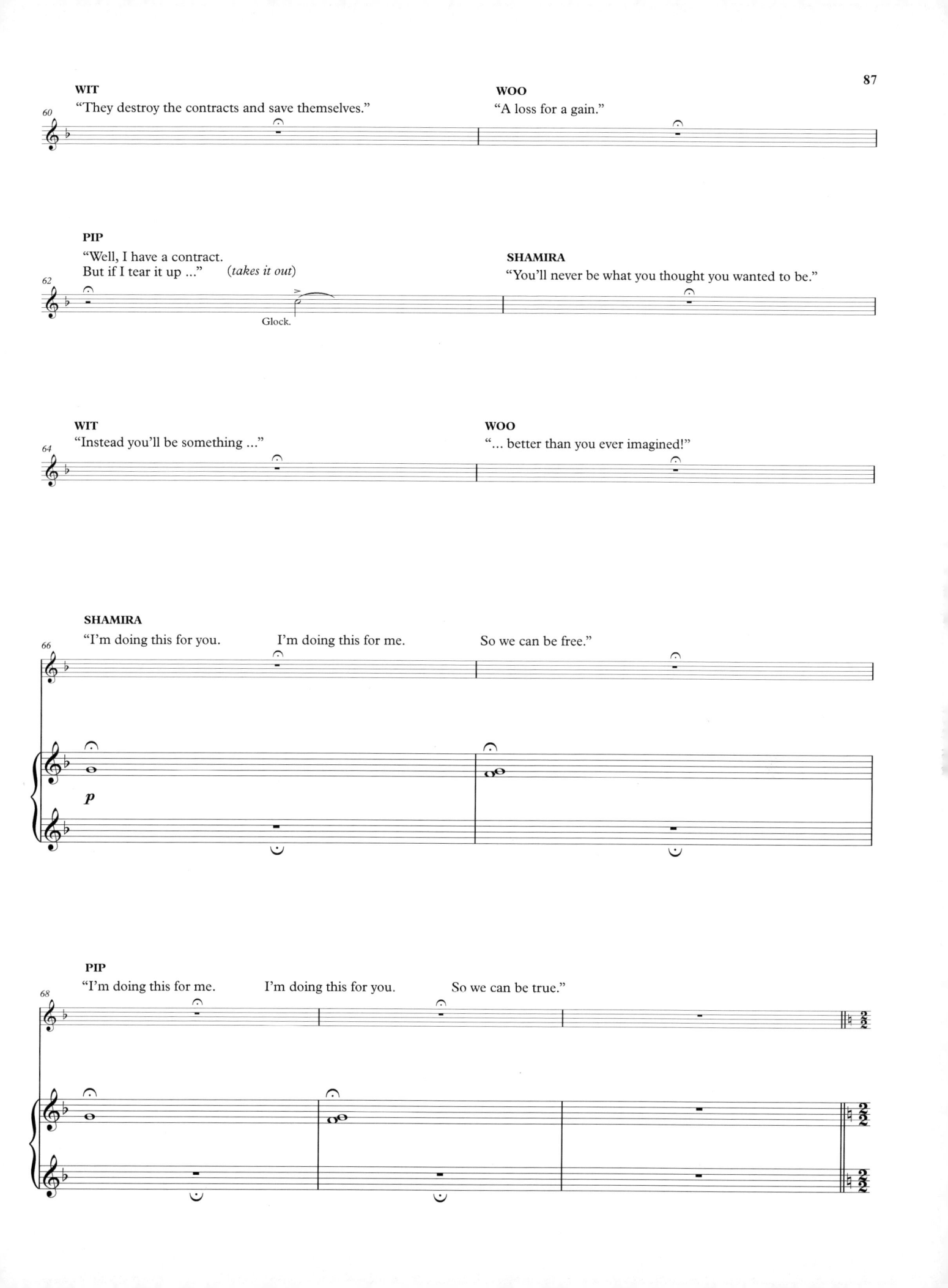
WIT
"They destroy the contracts and save themselves."
WOO
"A loss for a gain."
60
PIP
"Well, I have a contract.
But if I tear it up ..."
(takes it out)
Glock.
SHAMIRA
"You'll never be what you thought you wanted to be."
62
WIT
"Instead you'll be something ..."
WOO
"... better than you ever imagined!"
64
SHAMIRA
"I'm doing this for you.
I'm doing this for me.
So we can be free."
66
p
PIP
"I'm doing this for me.
I'm doing this for you.
So we can be true."
68

14. Dream Vision

(*Shamira, Pip*)

23
1.
whis-per in your ear,
I'm the same as you.
Fill-ing you with joy in-stead of fear.
25b
2.
Un-der-neath I'm like a spar-row too.
mf
Now, my luck-y
mf
30
spar-row, now you have the chance.
Wake up to the mu-sic and your
35
song will dance.
Time to be a he-ro, time to be a

40
star. Wake up now to who you real - ly are, you
45
real - ly are,
poco rit.
mp
you real - ly are.
mp
50
PIP p
a tempo
Like a fea-ther on the wind, like the dawn-ing of the day, I
(SHAMIRA)
a tempo
p
55
(PIP)
feel my song be - gin to play.
mp
From deep down with - in
mp

60
me, with - in me starts to shine a me - lo - dy that is com - plete - ly
65
(PIP)
mine. As each note falls in-to place,
SHAMIRA mp
I am your dream vi - sion come to tell you
70
I feel my song of light and grace. From
true. Lis - ten to the mu - sic deep in - side of you.

75
deep down with-in me, with - in me starts to shine a
Lis - ten to it whis - per, whis - per in your ear,
UNISON CHORUS and SATB CHORUS BIRDS slowly begin to gather on stage. They listen in amazement to the singing.
79
me - lo - dy that is com - plete - ly mine.
Fill - ing you with joy in - stead of fear.
83
mf
Now at last I can see it's true that I can
mf
Now, my luck - y spar - row, now you have the chance. Wake up to the
mf

88
sing, can sing as well as you. From deep with - in me
mu - sic and your song will dance. Time to be a he - ro,
93
starts to shine a song, a song that is com - plete - ly
time to be a star. Wake up now to who you real - ly are,
98
mine, com - plete - - ly mine.
you real - ly are.
mp

15. The Music of Light

(*Pip, Shamira, Unison Chorus Birds, SATB Chorus Birds, Highnote*)

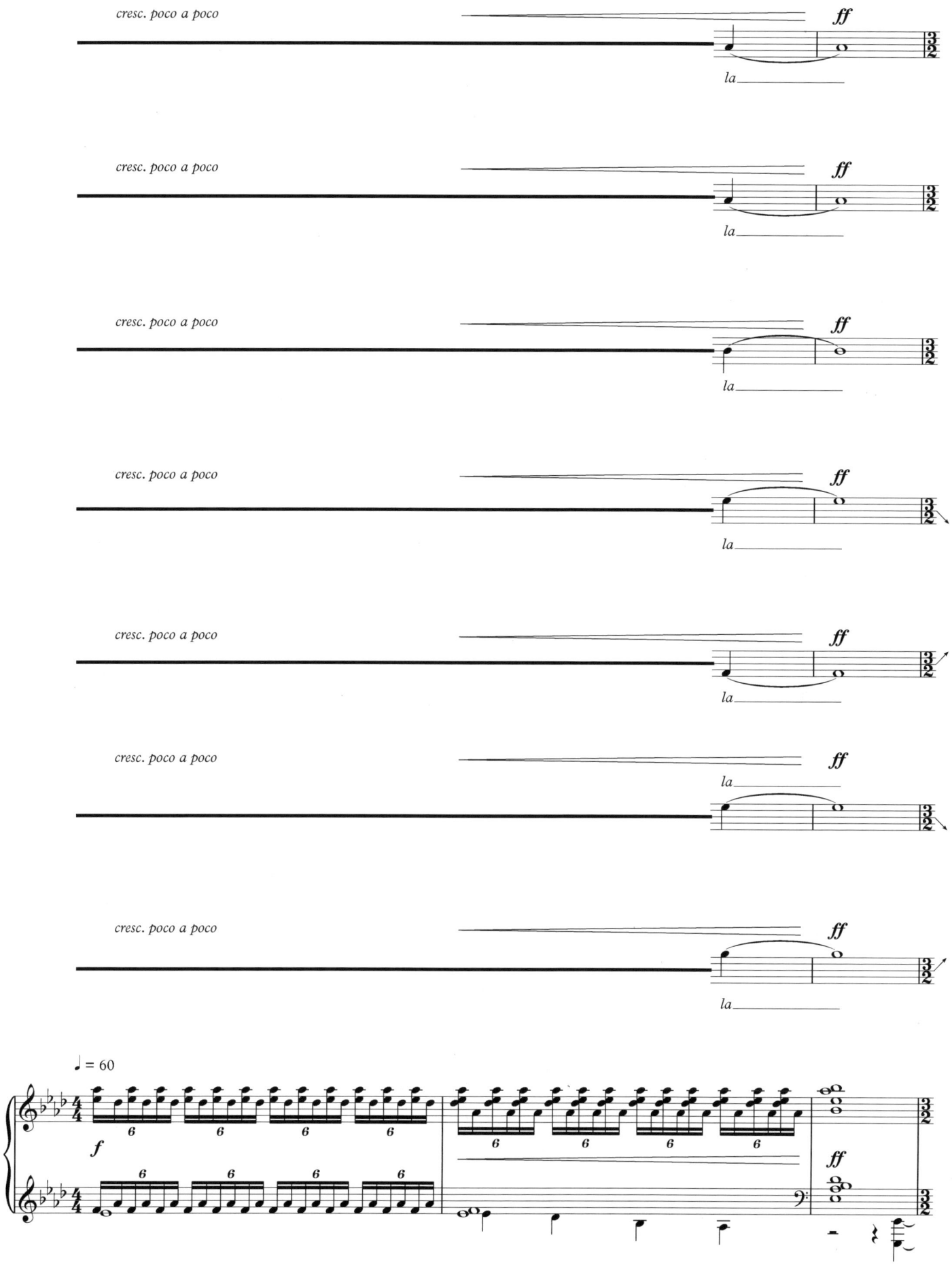
cresc. poco a poco
ff
la
cresc. poco a poco
ff
la
cresc. poco a poco
ff
la
cresc. poco a poco
ff
la
cresc. poco a poco
ff
la
cresc. poco a poco
ff
la
cresc. poco a poco
ff
la
♩ = 60
f
ff

6
Bright and strong ♩ = 100
UNIS.
f
By the fea-thers on our wing
S.
A.
f
By the fea-thers on our wing
T.
B.
f
Bright and strong ♩ = 100
f
9
Now we wake us up to sing.
Greet the sun and let it play
the mu - sic of light
Now we wake us up to sing.
Greet the sun and let it play
the mu - sic of light

12
on Mid - sum-mer's Day.
on Mid - sum-mer's Day.
15
Lis - ten to the hon-eyed sound
spill - ing on the sleep - y ground.
Lis - ten to the hon-eyed sound
spill - ing on the sleep - y ground.

17
Greet the sun and let it play the mu - sic of light
mu - sic of light
Greet the sun and let it play the mu - sic of light, of
19
on Mid - sum-mer's Day.
light on Mid - sum-mer's Day.
mf
This
mf

22
S.
A.
mu - sic so light and free,
mu - sic so light and free, sud - den - ly it dawns on me,
T.
B.
mf
24
f
O - pen your ears, it's not too late. Let ev - 'ry bird par -
f
f
27
-ti - ci - pate, par - ti - ci - pate.

30
UNIS.
f
By the fea-thers on our wing
Mu-sic needs us
S.
A.
f
By the fea-thers on our wing
Now we wake us up to sing.
T.
B.
f
33
all to sing, to sing the mu - sic of light,
Greet the sun and let it play the mu - sic of light on Mid - sum-mer's Day, the

HIGHNOTE (*sheds a tear*)

"That's the best dawn chorus I've ever heard. It makes me really proud to be a bird! Well done, everyone. I never thought I'd say this, but the dawn chorus isn't just for a few. It actually sounds better than ever before. From now on, everyone can sing. Well, I think we learnt a valuable lesson today ..."

ALL

"Oh do shut up!"

16. One Note (reprise)

(Unison Chorus Birds, SATB Chorus Birds)

8
let your song shine!
let your song shine!
To-
mf
mf
11
- day as you know is Mid-sum-mer's Day, when all the birds may have their say.
mf

13
f
Now we can tell you, life is good, We all sing in the neigh - bour-hood.
f
f

15
f
One note, to be-gin, let the light in. One note, now's the time,
One note, to be-gin, let the light in. One note, now's the time,

18
let your song shine!
let your song shine!
mf
We
mf
21
S.
A.
hear the beau - ty of your voice, we ce - le-brate, we all re-joice!
T.
B.
mf
23
f
Now we can tell you (not a word), all kinds of songs, they must be heard!
f
f

25
UNIS.
One note, to be-gin, let the light in. One note, now's the time,
S.
A.
One note, to be-gin, let the light in. One note, now's the time,
T.
B.
28
let your song, your song shine! One note, to be-gin,
let your song, your song shine! One note, to be-gin,
ff

31
let the light in. One note, now's the time, let your song
let the light in. One note, now's the time, let your song
34
shine! Let your song shine, let your
shine! Let your song shine, let your

All congratulate PIP as they depart to leave him alone on stage.
38
song
shine!
song
shine!
17. Epilogue
(Pip)
Moderate tempo ♩ = 84
PIP
p
7
p
All I real - ly came to show is how what lies be - neath can grow. And

9
how some-times the stran-gest mouth can let de-light-ful mu - sic out.
12
a little slower ♩ = 76
What-ev-er else you take a-way, re-
16
-mem-ber how we sang to-day. And in the si-lence of your heart,
19
rit.
let the heal-ing mu - sic
"Start."
(p)